D1133221

Date Due

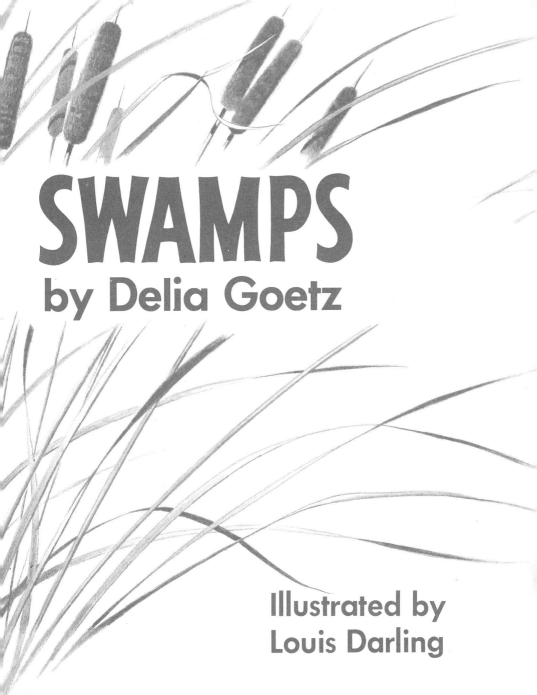

SWAMPS
by Delia Goetz

Illustrated by
Louis Darling

WILLIAM MORROW AND COMPANY   NEW YORK   1961

Swamps are low, spongy lands. There are
big swamps that stretch over thousands of
miles. There are small swamps no bigger than
a room. Some are thousands of years old, and
others are newly formed. Some have salt water,
and others have fresh water. Still others con-
tain both fresh and salt water. Whatever their
size or age or condition, swamps are wet lands.

3

Some swamps are part marsh and part bog. Marshes are low places covered with thin sheets of water. Bogs are swamplands in which moss and grass have decayed and been compressed into peat.

Every continent has swamps. Africa has more than any other. Asia has vast ones in Siberia, the lowlands near the Persian Gulf, and the great salt flats of India. Still others are in China, Malaya, and Indonesia. Europe, too, has swamps. Almost a third of Finland is swampland, and bogs or marshes cover parts of Great Britain. Even Australia, which is mostly desert, has swamps. They are also found in large parts of South America, Central America, and North America. The lowlands of the arctic tundra, which are frozen most of the year, become swamps during the summer thaw.

Swamps form when water cannot drain off lowlands. Usually this happens near large bodies of water, along low seacoasts, or near lakes and rivers. Water overflows, but the land is so low that it cannot drain off. Near the coast, tides wash into the fringe of plants and trees along the shore and form salt-water swamps.

Fresh-water swamps may be made by an overflowing river. After the spring rains fall, rivers rise and flood nearby lands. If the water cannot drain away, a swamp forms. Rivers also make swamps in another way. As a river nears its mouth, the current slows and the stream winds back and forth, forming a big horseshoe. Then the water may cut across the open end of the horseshoe. Plants begin to grow around the edge of the horseshoe-shaped stream and gradually spread toward the center. They hold soil and water, and finally a swamp forms.

Glaciers have also made swamps. The soil and rocks which they carried were left when the ice melted. This held water and kept it from draining away. Some hollows made by glaciers became swamps too.

Many swamps have been made by busy beavers. The dams they built across streams kept the water from draining away.

People often speak of swamps as wastelands. And many are. Most of them are too wet for farming. Often they are infested with millions of mosquitoes, gnats, termites, and other annoying or harmful insects. Poisonous reptiles live in the sluggish waters of tropical swamps, and animals dangerous to man make their homes in them or nearby.

But swamps may also be useful. Many plants and trees helpful to man grow in them. Animals that live there may provide us with food or hides or fur. Swamps are also places where plants and animals may be studied in their natural surroundings.

Although all swamps are wet places, not all of them look alike. Some have many trees. Some are a tangle of shrubs, bushes, and vines. Others have only grasses or tall, coarse reeds. The appearance of some swamps changes from season to season. Others look the same the year round.

THE EVERGLADES

Florida's swamps change little during the year. The Everglades of Florida, now a national park, is mostly swampland. Within it are two well-known swamps, the Big Cypress Swamp and the Corkscrew Swamp. All the year round grasses and other plants grow there. Pines and palms stand side by side.

Of all the trees that grow in the dimly lighted swamp the cypress is the most interesting. Its wide-spreading roots reach far out under the water, as if searching for a good place to anchor. From these roots grow the curious, bare, cone-shaped stumps known as cypress knees. Some people say the trees use the knees to breathe. Others believe the knees help to prop up the tree. They do not sprout leaves, nor do they become trees.

Mangrove trees that flourish in salt water grow in parts of Florida's swamps. Their roots push up like stilts and hold the trees out of the water. The branches send out aerial roots through which the tree breathes. These roots curve downward and thrust themselves into the mud. Bits of soil, shells of fish, and grasses

cling to them. Gradually so much soil piles
up at the bottom of the tree that it shuts off
the water. Then the tree dies.

Gray moss, sometimes known as old-man's-
beard, hangs from swamp trees like long,
thick veils. It needs neither water nor soil, for
it lives on air.

wood ibis

The fast-growing water hyacinth, which forms dense islands of green in the swamp waters, has a special way of living there. It breathes through a bulb that floats on the surface of the water.

Water lettuce, another fast-growing plant, gets along well in wet lands. In Florida's swamps, where it grows the year round, it forms a thick green carpet over the water. Neither strong arms on oars nor powerful engines can push a boat through a cover of thick water lettuce.

The swamps within the Everglades are a refuge to many birds. For some birds it is their year-round home; others spend only the winter there. The snowy egret is a year-round dweller and so is the large wood ibis, which is actually a stork. Both birds build their nests high in the tops of the cypress trees, away from harm.

snowy egret

The swamp is also the home of the speckled limpkin, so named because it walks with a limp. But it is the limpkin's cry that makes it best remembered. The Indians call it the crying bird; others describe its cry as sounding like the shout of a startled person. Usually there are also herons of many kinds, waiting patiently to catch fish for a meal.

Reptiles, too, live in the warm waters of Florida's swamps. The long brown object among the water lettuce may not be a stick but the snout of an alligator. He is waiting for his dinner of fish or turtle, both of which he prefers to man.

The deadly water moccasin is another reptile that lives in the Everglades. Its gleaming body slides silently through the water, then coils itself around a plant. Quickly its fangs may fasten into the finger of the person who stoops to pick a blossom.

raccoon

Animals that live on land in other places
make their homes in swamps here. Mischiev-
ous raccoons nibble a meal held in dainty
paws. The opossom, with a family of young

perched on its back, is there, and so is the grayish brown otter. Bobcats pick their way through the muck and mire. Timid white-tailed deer guide their fawns through the deep shadows.

otter

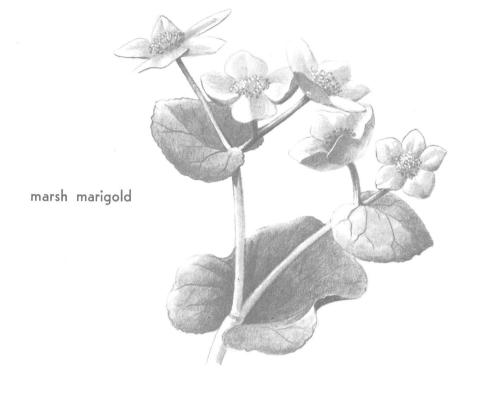

marsh marigold

SEASONS IN THE SWAMPS

Unlike the Everglades, the swamps or marshes in our Middle West change with the seasons. In spring, when the ice begins to melt, spears of green push up through the dry brown grass and patches of gray moss. Cattails begin to grow. Buds form on clumps of wild irises. The yellow blossoms of the marsh marigold brighten the swamp.

26

The bladderwort is one of the swamp's most unusual plants. Its long stems float on the water. Along the stems are little sacks, each with a door that swings inward. Later when the bladderwort is in blossom it lifts the blossoms above water. The empty bladder expands and sucks in water with a sudden rush. Water fleas sucked in with the water make a fine snack for the plant!

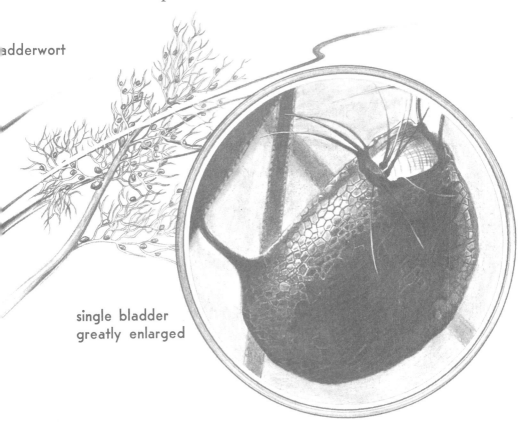

adderwort

single bladder
greatly enlarged

Not only plants but animals make their appearance in these swamps as spring comes. The muskrat moves out of his den, where he has spent the winter. The beaver starts his busy season of building. Salamanders and garter

muskrat

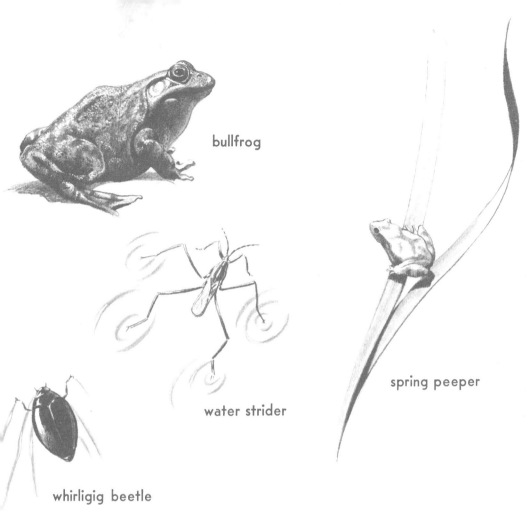

bullfrog

water strider

spring peeper

whirligig beetle

snakes slide along old logs that lie in the mud
and muck. Nimble frogs leap from place to
place, and solemn toads blink in the sunlight.
Turtles leave the mud at the bottom of the
swamp and poke their heads out of the water.
Black water bugs skim over the surface.

29

marsh wren

Spring also brings birds back to nest in the
swamps. Nest building is a busy, noisy time,
for the birds call and warble as they work.
The small brown wren weaves a neat nest,
round as a ball. The wood duck builds no
nest of its own, but moves into a hollow tree
and makes himself at home.

wood duck (male)

Ducks are well suited to living in swamps. Their webfeet serve them well in swimming, and natural oil keeps their feathers waterproof. Tiny sawlike edges around their broad flat bills help strain the food that they pick out of the water and mud.

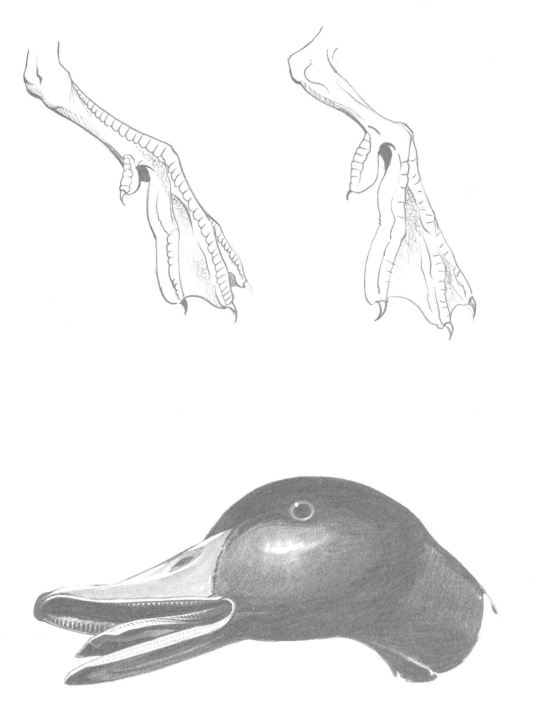

merganser

bufflehead

canvasback

Some ducks, such as the blue-green mallard, live in shallow water. Others, such as the canvasback and the black-and-white bufflehead, are diving ducks and prefer deeper waters. The red-breasted merganser is known as a fish duck, because it lives mostly on fish. This diet gives its flesh a fishy flavor, which many people dislike, and so hunters pass it up. Other ducks nest farther north and use the swamps of the Middle West as resting places along the way to and from their nesting ground.

duckweed

actual size

As the days grow warmer and summer appears, green scum floats on the water and duckweed forms thick mats, which look like little rafts. If rain is scarce, fish bones, pieces of floating weed, and decayed bits of waste are caught in the mud and the whole swamp has an unpleasant smell of rot and slime. Summer also brings buzzing, stinging swarms of unwelcome mosquitoes and other insects.

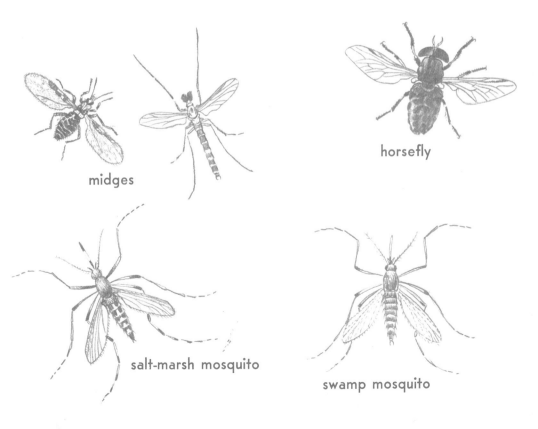

midges

horsefly

salt-marsh mosquito

swamp mosquito

In autumn new visitors come to the swamp. As the days grow shorter and colder, flocks of geese on their way south make their usual stopover. Wild ducks, too, swoop down for an overnight rest.

Soon winter comes. Now cold winds rustle the dry leaves of cattails and bulrushes, and snow drifts against their stalks. Ice forms on the water, and insects and fish burrow into the mud at the bottom of the swamp. Fish swim into passageways made by the muskrat. Hungry hawks hover over the swamp looking for a scurrying animal to pounce upon.

SWAMPS IN OTHER LANDS

Many plants and animals that live in the swamps of the United States also thrive in the wet lands of other countries. The tangled thickets of Finland's swamps are bright with the same blossoms and berries that grow in our northern swamps. Ducks, geese, and other migratory birds nest in the low bushes. Wild, fur-bearing animals roam over the land. Farther south in Europe hundreds of varieties of birds find refuge in the swamps of Spain.

A few plants can only be found in special swamps. Huge water lilies grow in the African Sudd. In the calm backwaters of the Amazon basin, in South America, the enormous water lily called the Victoria regia lives. Its huge flat leaves with turned-up edges look like enormous piepans, and they are so strong that a single leaf can support as much as sixty-five pounds. The lily's fragrant pink blossoms open only at night, and are soon replaced by round fruits filled with tasty seeds.

Papyrus also grows in the African Sudd. Long ago the Egyptians pressed the stalk of the papyrus into sheets of writing material on which they kept records. From the word *papyrus* we get the word *paper*. Papyrus shoots are also good food for the herds of cattle raised there.

papyrus

hippopotamus

Some animals unknown to our own swamps live in those of Africa and Asia. Among them are the bad-tempered rhinoceros and the clumsy hippotamus that love to wallow in swampy places.

Animals that roam near the Sudd use it for a watering place. Herds of neatly striped zebra clatter along on small hoofs. Gazelles look about to make certain that no leopard or lion is near before stopping to drink. Long-necked giraffes seem to tangle their long legs as they run across the swamp, ever on the alert for fierce animals.

Indian rhinoceros

HOMES IN THE SWAMPS

Most swamps are better homes for plants and animals than they are for man. The Seminole Indians are the only people who have made their home in the Everglades. They settled there more than a hundred years ago, when they were fleeing from the white men. Now they know every plant, animal, and corner of the swamps as well as they know each other.

The Seminole get their food by hunting
and fishing. Often they gather herbs that are
used to make medicine and sell them to get
some money. They build their *chickees,* as their
homes are called, two feet above the water.
The roofs are made of leaves of the huge cab-
bage palmetto. The houses stand in small villages. People curious to see how the Seminole
live pay to enter their villages and look
around. But the Seminole are not friendly
hosts and have little to say to such visitors.

Slowly the Seminole are adopting modern
ways. Now most of them have given up their
canoes made of cypress logs and use air boats.
The air boat has an airplane propeller turned

by a motor, and it can float on shallow water.
Some Seminole travel in a swamp buggy,
which is either a jeep or an automobile fitted
with enormous rubber tires.

In some ways the people who live in the African swamps lead much the same life as the Seminole do. Those who live in the swamps of the Congo River move about in dugout canoes. Some of the canoes are so large that forty or fifty people are needed to paddle them. These people are fishermen, but also weave baskets with which they trap fish.

The people who live in the swamps of the Sudd, along the Nile River, are cattlemen. They burn off the old papyrus beds so that the cattle may eat the fresh green shoots that then spring up. The Sudd dweller rarely kills his cattle for meat. He likes to have a big herd to show that he is a wealthy man.

Life is hard for the marsh dwellers of Iraq, who live on the other side of the world from our own swamplands. In winter the swamps of Iraq are damp and cold. In summer they are hot and humid, and mosquitoes buzz around them. Even worse are the wild boars that live there. They have tusks as sharp as razors and can destroy the crops and also the men who tend them.

The swamp dwellers of Iraq, like those everywhere, depend upon the swamp for their food and building materials. From the tall, stiff reeds that grow in the swamp they build their arched homes. They group them together to form villages, which stand on several layers of reed-mat platforms. The swamp dweller's work-day begins and ends in the reed beds. Some collect dried reeds for making mats.

Others pick fresh green shoots to feed the buffaloes. From the buffalo the people get milk, cheese, and leather. Now and then a trader paddles his boat into the swamp, bringing grain and cloth to trade for the finely woven reed mats that the swamp people make.

Life for these swamp dwellers is not all
hard work. When the day's work is done they
like to visit each other, and they sing and
dance to the music of the drum and tambour-
ine. Even as they work in the reed beds they
sing and laugh, as people do everywhere.

The people who live in the peat bogs of Ireland have a very different life from those who live in the marshes of Iraq. The bog dwellers live in stone cottages with thatched roofs. Nearby are the peat bogs from which men cut big pieces of peat, called turf. Turf makes a warm fire that burns so slowly that people in Ireland say it lasts from one year's end to another.

The cowboys who live on big, swampy Marajó, an island at the mouth of the Amazon River, travel by dugout canoe, on horseback, or astride lumbering oxen. They live on meat and fish, and a kind of bread made from the roots of manioc. The houses are raised on stilts over the swampy ground. For fun the cowboys lasso crocodiles in the shallow pools left in the pastures.

SAVING THE SWAMPS

Many lands that were once swamps have been drained or filled in. Nowhere have people done this so successfully as in the Netherlands. The name itself means lowlands. Many fields, which are fertile now, were once swamp-

land that was often flooded by the waters of the North Sea.

The story of how the Dutch made these lowlands into productive fields is a long one. It took years to build canals and dikes, and then pump the water out and wash the salt from the soil. Since then other nations, such as England, Italy, and France, have called on the Dutch to help them drain their swamps.

There are different reasons why people have drained swamplands. Some were drained to fight diseases caused by insects that lived in them. Because swamps were considered unpleasant places in which to live, and harmful to health, many people thought that unless they were drained the land was worthless.

Other swamps were drained to make new land. As our country grew and more land was needed, men drained swamps or filled them to

make room for more farms and factories, more
roads and airports. Few men thought that it
might also be harmful to get rid of swamps.
But as they disappeared other things happened.
There were both more floods and more
droughts than before. There were also more
fires, for swamps had acted as firebreaks.
Hunters noticed that there was less wild game.
Wildlife that once lived in the swamps was
dying out, because it had no place to live.

Today only about a fourth of the lands that were once swamps, marshes, or bogs remain. Now people realize that these wet lands are not wastelands, but are valuable for many reasons. Our government is buying many of the lands that were once swamps in order to keep them as they were. A number of them, like the Everglades of Florida, have been made into national parks.

Now we know that swamps and other wet lands are needed to help preserve wildlife. And swamplands are important to man, too. Not only do they help protect him from fire, flood, and drought, but they offer him places where he can enjoy wilderness as unspoiled as it was when men first found it.